PRESENTED BY

WESTMINSTER SCHOOLS

SMYTHE GAMBRELL
LIBRARY

THE SEARCH FOR
SEISMOSAURUS
THE WORLD'S LONGEST DINOSAUR

J. Lynett Gillette · *paintings by* Mark Hallett

Dial Books for Young Readers New York

To Jennifer and David J.L.G.
To my mother, with love M.H.

Published by Dial Books for Young Readers
A Division of Penguin Books USA Inc.
375 Hudson Street
New York, New York 10014

Library of Congress Cataloging in Publication Data
Gillette, J. Lynett.
The search for Seismosaurus: the world's longest dinosaur / by J. Lynett Gillette ;
paintings by Mark Hallett.—1st ed. p.   cm.
Includes index.
Summary: Documents the discovery and excavation of Seismosaurus,
the longest dinosaur ever found, and reconstructs its appearance and habitat.
ISBN 0-8037-1358-4—ISBN 0-8037-1359-2 (lib. bdg.)
1. Seismosaurus—Juvenile literature [1. Seismosaurus. 2. Dinosaurs. 3. Paleontology. 4. Fossils.]
I. Hallett, Mark, 1947–   ill. II. Title.
QE862.S3G55 1994   567.9'7—dc20   92-28199   CIP   AC

Mark Hallett's paintings are rendered in gouache.

Many people worked with me to tell the story of *Seismosaurus*. Cindy Kane,
my editor, asked the right questions and kept the book going with her encourage-
ment and enthusiasm. David Gillette gave inspiration, helpful suggestions, and much
support. In addition, I would like to thank Wilson and Peggy Bechtel, the staff at
Ghost Ranch, the Southwest Paleontology Foundation, Los Alamos National
Laboratory, the National Geographic Society, the National Science Foundation, and
the Martin Marietta Corporation; and to acknowledge the efforts of hundreds of
volunteers and many others. This book is possible because of their dedication
to the search for *Seismosaurus*. J.L.G.

Some people imagine that great scientific discoveries begin and end in a flash, in an exciting moment when a lucky scientist says, "Aha, that's it!" But the discovery of a new dinosaur fossil is only the first step in a long search for clues.

Paleontologists, the scientists who study ancient life, need time to answer questions when they find bones, teeth, tracks, or other remains buried in the ground. What do these remains, or fossils, tell about an animal that has been dead for thousands or millions of years?

The search for Seismosaurus, the world's longest dinosaur, has been going on for many years, and the excitement isn't over yet.

THE DISCOVERY

It all began on a warm spring day in 1979. Jan Cummings and Arthur Loy set out to explore and hike in the beautiful high desert country near Albuquerque, New Mexico.

View of mesa country from *Seismosaurus* site

4

Near the end of the day, the two friends stopped on a high, flat-topped mountain. On that mesa they discovered petroglyphs, or rock carvings, on a sandstone rock. With their fingers they traced the shapes of snakes, lizards, humans, and lightning bolts. Hundreds of years earlier, Native American artists had carved that rock with stone tools.

Petroglyphs made by Native American artists

As Cummings and Loy started to climb down to the valley, they saw something unusual buried in the sandstone. Bones, thought the hikers. Something big had once lived here—perhaps even a dinosaur.

Just in case the discovery was important, the hikers returned in a few days with friends and took photographs of the bones. Later the hikers showed the photos to a paleontologist. He believed the sandstone on the mesa was so hard that no one would ever be able to get any fossils out of that ground.

A friend of the hikers with fossils in sandstone on mesa

Very discouraged, the hikers went back to the mesa and gently covered the bones with sand. They wanted to protect the skeleton from sun and rain, and from people who might cut up the fossil to make jewelry.

Fortunately, the story did not end there. Six years later, in the spring of 1985, Cummings and Loy were hiking in the desert again when they crossed onto the same mesa where they had found the rock carvings and the fossil bones. Wind and water had carried some of the sand away, but the bones were still safe. No one had moved them.

The hikers decided to try again to tell a scientist about the bones. They gave new photographs to a friend, Frank Walker, who said he could find a paleontologist who would look at them.

He took the pictures to a new museum of natural history that was being built in Albuquerque. Paleontologist David Gillette was working at the museum to get ready for the grand opening. Some days he helped create life-sized dinosaur sculptures with artist Dave Thomas. Other days he fitted

Albertosaurus (sculpted by Dave Thomas) in front of the New Mexico Museum of Natural History in Albuquerque

together skeletons for the museum's room full of dinosaurs from New Mexico.

"Fantastic," said David Gillette when Walker laid the photos on his desk. He could tell that the bones were from the tail of a very large plant-eating dinosaur, perhaps *Diplodocus*. But *Diplodocus* had never been found in New Mexico. Gillette was very curious to know if there was a new dinosaur

David Gillette

that should be added to the *Stegosaurus*, *Camarasaurus*, *Allosaurus*, and *Camptosaurus* in the museum's large dinosaur hall. All the dinosaurs in that room lived in New Mexico between 150 and 144 million years ago, during the Jurassic Period of the earth's history.

Gillette and Walker made plans to see the bones and perhaps get them out of the ground.

8

Camptosaurus

Stegosaurus

Camarasaurus

Allosaurus

Jurassic Period Dinosaurs of New Mexico

THE FIRST DAY OF DIGGING

By mid-June of 1985 Gillette had permission to dig from the land-owners, the United States Bureau of Land Management. The temperature was near 100° F (38° C) and a swarm of tiny biting gnats called "no-see-ums" attacked the field crew as they began work.

The first day; in the center of the photo are the exposed tail bones of the dinosaur.

Gillette was anxious to get the bones free of the sandstone so that he could see their shape and size. Each bone was connected to the next just as it had been in the living animal. Hammers and chisels slowly cut the bones out of the rock one by one. They appeared to be backbones, or vertebrae, from the tail.

The vertebrae were wrapped in strips of burlap that had been soaked in plaster and water. When the plaster was hard, five people carried each heavy bone, eight in all, up the hill to a waiting pickup truck.

Newspaper and plaster protected the bones during travel.

It was impossible not to be excited about the bones. Whichever dinosaur they belonged to, it certainly was big!

Gillette knew the bones belonged to a member of the group of giant plant-eating dinosaurs called sauropods. Many sauropods such as *Camarasaurus*, *Apatosaurus*, *Diplodocus*, *Brachiosaurus*, and the super giants *Ultrasaurus* and *Supersaurus* lived in the Jurassic Period, which lasted from about 208 million years ago to 144 million years ago.

But of all those sauropods only *Camarasaurus* had been found in New Mexico. To which dinosaur did the new bones belong? Gillette needed time for study.

There was no doubt that the bones belonged to a dinosaur that lived in the Jurassic Period. At the dig Gillette had recognized the tan-colored sandstone as coming from a time late in the Jurassic when the sand was being laid down by rivers and streams. Other geologists who studied the dinosaur site suggested a date of 150 million years ago for these rocks.

Flowing river in Jurassic times. Two *Allosaurus* investigate *Seismosaurus* skeleton.

The excavators wondered why they hadn't found more of the dinosaur. They found the tail. What happened to the rest of the animal? They had several ideas about this.

After the giant dinosaur died, some of the skeleton may have been buried in sand along the side of a flowing river. Maybe tail vertebrae, which were not as heavy as the rest of the bones, had been swept downstream to be discovered millions of years later.

Or maybe *Allosaurus* and other meat-eating dinosaurs carried away all the tastier parts of the skeleton, leaving behind only the tail.

A third idea was even more exciting. Maybe the rest of the animal was still lying nearby, just out of reach of the diggers' shovels. But to look for more of the dinosaur, the excavators would need more time, more money, and more ideas about where to dig.

NAMING DAY

Another year went by while museum technicians worked to clean the hard sandstone from the bones. One evening at home in his cabin in the woods, David Gillette decided it was time to name this new discovery.

After much study of the bones he was sure the dinosaur belonged to the same family as *Diplodocus,* but it was different enough to need a new scientific name. The spines on the vertebrae of the new animal were very straight and tall, pointing up to the sky. In *Diplodocus,* these spines leaned backward toward the tip of the tail.

Scientists all over the world use Latin and Greek names for living and fossil animals. Each animal's scientific name has two parts, first the *genus* name and then the *species* name. The two names used together describe an animal that is clearly different from all other animals.

How about a name for the dinosaur that mentioned its enormous size? Judging by the size of the tail bones, this animal was at least 150 feet long—certainly the longest dinosaur ever found. It was almost as long as four school buses placed end to end! But other large dinosaurs already had the names *Supersaurus* and *Ultrasaurus.*

For a moment he considered "Superdupersaurus." He closed his eyes and imagined this animal walking. The ground would shake when the dinosaur took a step, as if an earthquake's seismic waves had arrived. That was it! *Seismosaurus,* the "earthshaker" dinosaur, had the first part of its name.

For the species name Gillette decided to honor his good friends, Jim and Ruth Hall, who had taught many people about fossils and had helped paleontologists dig dinosaurs at their home on nearby Ghost Ranch. The name was now complete: *Seismosaurus halli.*

Gillette knew from his studies of dinosaur tracks that these sauropods traveled in herds, perhaps like elephants do today. He invented a new way of measuring the weight of these giant dinosaurs by comparing them to the size of elephants.

Artist Mark Hallett's reconstructed view of *Seismosaurus*. In the foreground is *Dryosaurus*, a small dinosaur that has been found in the western United States.

The Longest Dinosaurs

Ultrasaurus
estimated 60 feet tall, 100 feet long

Seismosaurus
estimated 150 feet long

All these dinosaurs lived in the Jurassic Period of the earth's history. Since both *Ultrasaurus* and *Supersaurus* are known from only a few bones each, their lengths are rough educated guesses. A human is included for size comparison only, as humans and dinosaurs did not live on the earth at the same time.

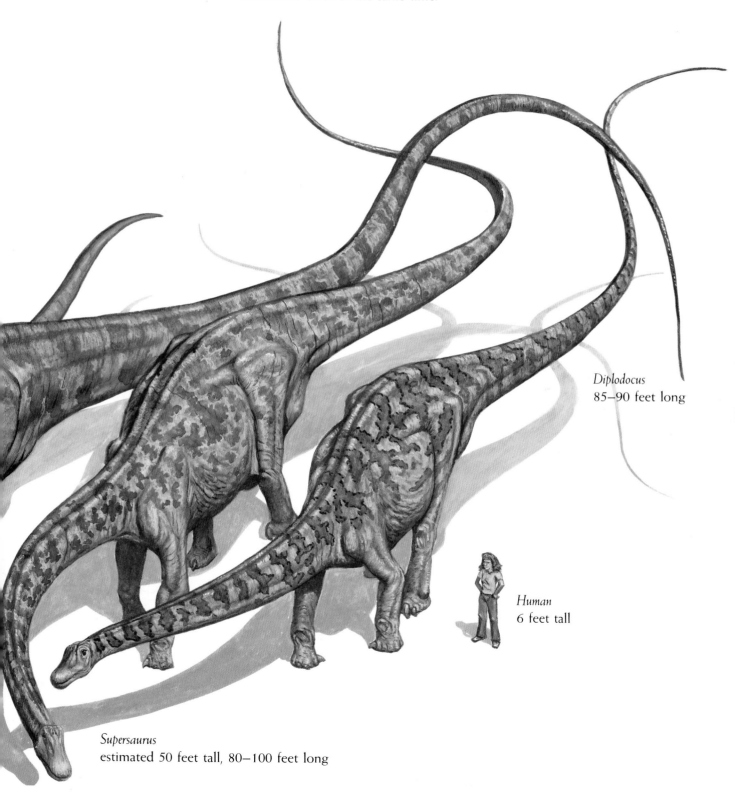

Diplodocus
85–90 feet long

Human
6 feet tall

Supersaurus
estimated 50 feet tall, 80–100 feet long

One large elephant might weigh 10,000 pounds. How many elephants would weigh the same as one 87-foot-long *Diplodocus*? About six. How many elephants would equal one *Seismosaurus*? About ten! One *Seismosaurus*, then, would equal ten EEUs (Equivalent Elephant Units). That was almost 100,000 pounds, or 50 tons.

HELP

David Gillette wasn't satisfied yet. He had studied the eight tail bones of the new dinosaur. He had given it a new name.

But what if there were still more bones in the ground?

Gillette knew that any digging at the dinosaur site would be hard work. Sandstone is very heavy. Every cubic foot of this rock (which would fill a box one foot wide, one foot long, and one foot deep) weighs 125 pounds.

An early reconstruction of *Seismosaurus* by artist Doug Henderson, drawn on the basis of the first season's excavation

How could the excavators move as little sandstone as possible to look for the rest of the skeleton? Besides wanting to save work, Gillette wanted to protect the great natural beauty of the mesa.

When a group of scientists from Los Alamos National Laboratory (LANL) came to the *Seismosaurus* site one day, Gillette shared his problems with them.

"Is there a way we could see underground? We'd like to know exactly where to dig next," he said.

The visiting scientists promised to bring out some of their new sensing machines to look for dinosaur bones under the ground.

Gillette had more questions for his visitors. He wanted to know exactly what had happened to the bones of the *Seismosaurus* when it died. Were the fossil bones he discovered still bone or had they slowly changed to stone after they were buried? Was stone all that remains of an animal after millions of years? Perhaps careful study could find "ghosts" left behind of the soft parts of the animal's bone. These "ghosts" could be any bits of the actual building blocks of life, the proteins.

The scientists agreed to look for clues about the body of the *Seismosaurus*. They had lots of good ideas.

LEARNING TO SEE UNDERGROUND

David Gillette was encouraged by the enthusiasm of the LANL scientists. Soon the National Geographic Society gave money to help the project continue. Now Gillette could buy plaster and hammers and chisels for his many volunteers.

In 1987 Gillette and a crew drove from Albuquerque to the *Seismosaurus* site. They all hoped that a little more digging would uncover the rest of the dinosaur's tail. The eight bones excavated earlier had been from near the middle of the tail. The tip could not be found. Wind, rain, and sun— the forces of erosion—had probably broken and washed away bones closest to the mesa's edge.

Sure enough, after working slowly through the sandstone with picks, shovels, brushes, hammers, and chisels, the crew did find more of the

David Gillette uncovering *Seismosaurus* bones, 1987

dinosaur. First another tail vertebra, then another, and another appeared. During the next few months, more tail vertebrae were uncovered. Counting the eight that had already been found, they now had a total of nineteen bones from the tail.

The excavators were working toward the dinosaur's head. But as the crew dug, the line of connected bones turned into the steep wall of rock at the mesa's edge. Where to dig next? They weren't sure.

The time had come to try LANL's new instruments for looking into the earth.

One of these instruments, a magnetometer, had recently helped locate the wreck of a Spanish ship buried at the bottom of the Atlantic Ocean. With a few changes to his magnetometer, the technician was ready to help search for *Seismosaurus* beneath the mesa.

The magnetometer measures very small changes in the earth's magnetic field. The earth behaves like a giant magnet, sending out strong lines of magnetic forces from the North and South Poles. These forces pass over all the earth. When magnetic waves travel through large objects such as mountains, the waves are bent. The LANL scientists hoped that they could measure the bend in magnetic forces passing through something as small as a bone.

Mineralogist Phil Vergamini ready to measure magnetic waves
at the *Seismosaurus* site with his magnetometer

The scientists walked in straight lines across the whole mesa and back again. On their map they marked the measurements from the magnetometer.

Phil Vergamini recording magnetic waves with his dog, Coalbin

Other scientists from Sandia National Laboratory and LANL joined in the dinosaur hunt. They brought a radar instrument that rested on a sled. Two people held the sled's handles and walked back and forth over all of the mesa. The radar sent waves of energy into the ground. Sandstone layers below the surface reflected the waves back to the radar receiver.

A radar instrument with waves that can pass beneath the earth's surface is carried over the *Seismosaurus* site.

Whenever the radar waves passed through something thicker or harder than the rest of the sandstone, the waves took longer to be bounced back up to the surface. Computers recorded patterns of the returning radar waves. Any waves that came back more slowly than the rest might be clues about dinosaur bones.

Returning radar waves are received by the mobile computer at the site.

THE BIG TEST

Soon the scientists decided to put their ideas to a test. They would drill a few holes in the sandstone to check for bones. They put red flags on the ground at spots that seemed best for finding bones according to their maps. One place looked especially good for drilling because it was a promising spot on both the magnetometer and the ground-radar maps.

By now word of the unusual dinosaur excavation had attracted attention from television producers. David Gillette invited one film company to be present on the drilling days, the days of the Big Test.

A huge drilling truck was driven to the site from Los Alamos National

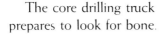
The core drilling truck prepares to look for bone.

24

Laboratory. The men who operated the drilling truck would cut long plugs of earth called cores from several test sites. Everyone hoped that the cores would be filled with bones.

When the drilling truck was parked, the core-cutting pipe was lowered to the ground. The test began. Everyone tried to stay calm as the pipe cut deeper and deeper into the earth. Twenty feet down was far enough.

Drilling for dinosaur bone

The drillers pulled the core up out of the earth and laid it in the back of a pickup truck. Everyone pushed forward to see what had been brought out of the ground. Sandstone, bits of silt, bits of clay, and more sandstone. No bone anywhere. Everyone sighed. They would have to try again.

Now for the test hole that held the most promise of bone. The drillers set to work while everyone paced to the steady hum of the twisting, cutting pipe. Again the men pulled the core out of the earth and laid it on the pickup. As the scientists held their breath, geologist Hilde Schwartz looked at the core. Sandstone, silt, sandstone, silt, clay, sandstone, sandstone. No bone? Schwartz went back over the core again. No bone. Everyone had hoped for better news.

Center, Geologist Hilde Schwartz looks for dinosaur bone in a core sample.

The drilling kept on for the rest of the day and the next, but there was no bone in any of the cores.

The television crew, hoping to film an exciting story, had to settle for an ordinary day in the scientists' lives. A small bit of stubborn hope kept everyone working in spite of the disappointments. Each disappointment taught them how to run a better test next time.

LEARNING TO SEE VERY SMALL

While scientists were testing for *Seismosaurus* at the site, new work on this dinosaur began in laboratories. Chemists, geologists, mineralogists, and physicists were looking very closely at the bones. They all wanted to have a better understanding of what happens to an animal when it dies and is buried for a very long time. How do bones change when they are buried for 150 million years?

To begin the new studies, Hilde Schwartz sliced a piece of bone so thin that she could see light through it. She first glued the bone to a piece of glass, then put the glass under the lens of a microscope. She saw colorful mineral crystals such as calcite, quartz, and hematite. The minerals grew only in empty spaces where soft tissues had once been, before the animal died. The bone had not changed to stone. Instead, as time passed, the bone

A thin piece of *Seismosaurus* bone with small grains of sandstone as seen with the microscope. *Right,* The minerals quartz and hematite; *left,* bone cells

Seismosaurus bone under the microscope, with small rounded mineral fragments of quartz and calcite filling empty spaces in the bone

had simply added some extra "stone," or minerals. That is why very old fossils feel heavier than bones of modern animals.

Schwartz could also see the tiny round bone cells. Even their smallest details were clear. They looked no different than bone cells in living animals. After 150 million years in the ground, the bone was still bone.

Oval-shaped *Seismosaurus* bone cells under the microscope

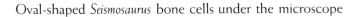

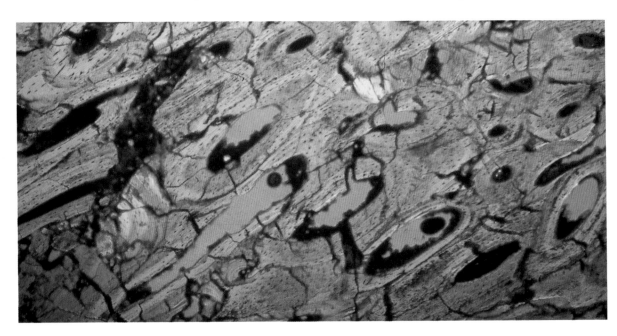

Several chemists agreed that *Seismosaurus* bone was almost exactly the same as bone from an ordinary cow. Seventy important elements that are found in cow bone, such as carbon, hydrogen, and phosphorus, were also found in the dinosaur's bone.

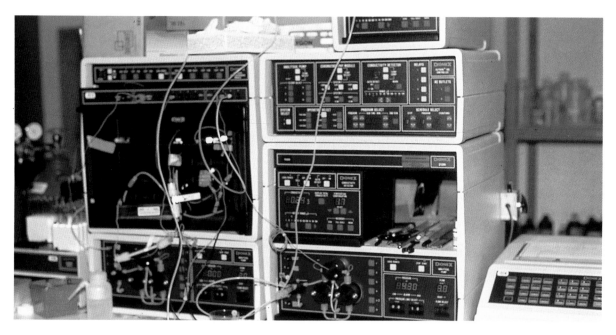

Equipment at Los Alamos National Laboratory (LANL) where the dinosaur bone is analyzed for its elements such as carbon and hydrogen

Another scientist, mineralogist Phil Vergamini, planned to study the mineral called apatite. This is the mineral that makes bone strong enough to support great weights. Apatite crystals are known to have only one shape in living bone.

Being buried under many tons of earth for a long time would probably change the crystals' shape, thought Vergamini. He did an experiment to look at very small particles of apatite crystals—the actual molecules of the crystal.

In the laboratory he put a small cube of *Seismosaurus* bone into the neutron scattering accelerator. At high speed, the accelerator pushed neutrons (particles from the center of atoms) along a tunnel. When the neutrons hit the *Seismosaurus* bone apatite, some were bounced away, or reflected. The patterns the reflected neutrons made showed Vergamini the exact shape of the mineral crystals. The crystals were shaped the same as those in a cow bone.

It was a great surprise to learn that the *Seismosaurus* bone apatite was not different at all from bone apatite in living animals.

Seismosaurus hip bone with holes where small samples have been removed for laboratory testing

That was good news. If *Seismosaurus* bone was much the same today as it was when the dinosaur lived, maybe there was hope for finding traces of the soft parts of the dinosaur bone—the proteins. All living tissue is made of proteins. Collagen is one protein that makes bone flexible, so that a rib, for example, can bend each time an animal breathes.

Dale Spall and other chemists began a project that was to last for several years. They crushed small samples of *Seismosaurus* bone and dissolved them in different liquids. Over and over they searched the liquids for proteins. They wanted to be especially careful not to be fooled by unwanted proteins that might accidentally be present in the samples. Plant roots growing near the *Seismosaurus* bones might have added plant proteins that could be mistaken for dinosaur proteins.

Finally, in 1991, the chemists were ready to share what they had learned. Yes, they announced, they had found bits of several dinosaur proteins. Even the living tissue in bone was not entirely lost! This was an impressive discovery. Next the scientists will look for ways to identify exactly which of the many kinds of proteins in a living animal were found in the dinosaur bone.

MORE DIGGING AND LOOKING UNDERGROUND

Back at the *Seismosaurus* site David Gillette and his field assistants, Peggy Bechtel and Wilson Bechtel, had continued to dig. Dozens of volunteers picked up shovels, hammers, and chisels and moved more sandstone. Connected to the tail vertebrae, they found five hip vertebrae with attached hip bones.

Wilson Bechtel adds plaster over the hip bones in the dinosaur quarry.

Each time bones were removed, there were new problems to solve. The hip bones were tremendously heavy; one block of bone weighed about 4,000 pounds. By the end of 1987, the nineteen tail vertebrae, five hip

Left to right: Jennifer, David, and
Lynett Gillette after a day's work
of plastering on the hip bones

vertebrae, and five of the hip bones were out of the ground.

When the ground warmed in the spring of 1988, the excavators began
digging again. Months passed and no new bones appeared.

The large block containing the hip bones
is ready to be lifted out of the quarry.

In the meantime a new instrument was being tested at the dinosaur site. A physicist from Oak Ridge National Laboratory in Tennessee thought that sound waves might help to find more bones from *Seismosaurus*.

Alan Witten planned to use a special shotgun that could shoot a bullet into the earth. He was dinosaur hunting, not with a bullet, but with the sound waves that were made by the bullet. He placed sound recorders into the old core holes that had been dug earlier on the days of the disappointing test. Each recorder was connected to the computer in the back of his car.

Every time Witten pulled the trigger, the traveling sound waves were picked up by the recorders below the ground and saved by the computer. If the waves of sound hit something harder than sandstone, they would travel faster.

Alan Witten with his equipment for measuring underground sound waves. Flags will mark testing locations; the computer in the back of his car will receive the signals from the sensors put into the core holes.

Using "Betsy," a modified shotgun, to pound the earth and create sound waves to look for bones

It wasn't long before the numbers on the computer told Witten that something besides sandstone was resting beneath the mesa. He thought he probably had found bone. But, oddly, the best numbers came from the same

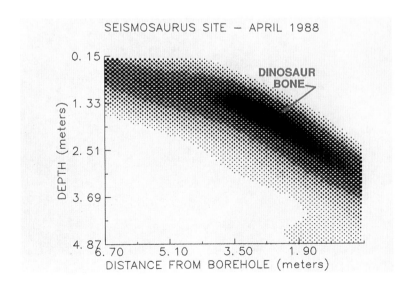

A computer printout of a possible dinosaur bone

place in the ground where all the other scientists had also thought there should be bone—the place where the cores drilled in the earth had found no bone. Witten was puzzled.

While Witten kept studying the sound wave patterns, the excavators kept on digging. That summer they uncovered eight vertebrae from the middle of the body, each with rib bones attached, up to the neck. During the next

The eight vertebrae from the mid-body are ready for plastering.

four years, four neck vertebrae were also discovered, bringing the total to thirty-two vertebrae by 1992. By then volunteers had moved over one million pounds of sandstone. When the project was over, the crew planned to put all the sand back in the hole.

A ROCKY DIET

Peggy and Wilson Bechtel found a heap of shiny rocks under one of the dinosaur's vertebrae at the beginning of the neck. All of the rocks were much larger than the tiny grains of sandstone found everywhere else at the site. Many of the rocks were the size of large marbles. Some were as large as plums.

The dinosaur diggers had seen such round rocks once before. When the *Seismosaurus'* hip bones were uncovered, the digging crew collected dozens of smooth round rocks from under the ribs. This was the position where the stomach would have been. David Gillette believed those rocks were gastroliths, or "stomach stones" that were smoothed by being ground together with food and acid in the dinosaur's belly. A geologist was already studying those round rocks to see if she could see differences between them and ones smoothed by river water.

A pile of stomach stones (gastroliths) from *Seismosaurus*

Gastroliths were not a new discovery. Other paleontologists had found polished stones with the skeletons of other large plant-eating dinosaurs.

The surprise for Gillette was finding gastroliths in two places—in the stomach area and in the place where the neck joins the body. He looked at living birds for the answer to this puzzle. His daughter Jennifer's pet cockatiel had a crop, a pouch at the end of its throat, which it filled with tiny pebbles. It also had a gizzard at the end of its stomach that stored pebbles for more food grinding. *Seismosaurus* may have had both a crop and a gizzard for grinding plants, just as birds have today.

Another dinosaur's tooth was later discovered near the stomach stones. *Allosaurus*, the ancestor of *Tyrannosaurus*, may have taken a bite of the already dead *Seismosaurus* and knocked out a tooth on one of the gastroliths.

Seismosaurus probably ate and traveled in herds with others of its kind, much as elephants do today.

THE VERTEBRA WITH A HOLE

One morning Peggy Bechtel happened to look down into one of the old core holes. She remembered the disappointing core removed from the hole—the one everyone had thought would have bone. The sunlight shone at just the right angle for Peggy to see down into the narrow hole. She was sure she saw something besides sandstone. It might be worth digging there.

She and Wilson Bechtel dug until they touched bone. In a few days they had uncovered a new vertebra. When the sand was cleared from the bone, everyone saw a sight they would never forget.

The vertebra had a v-shaped spine on its upper side, and right between the natural split in the "v" was the core hole dug months earlier! The drillers had missed the vertebra entirely by fitting the core neatly into a natural open space in the bone.

The vertebra with a hole

Maybe the instruments that looked under the ground were working better than anyone dared to believe! Scientists could continue their underground studies with new hope.

WHAT NEXT?

*S*eismosaurus' bones are now in many different laboratories. The men and women who have studied *Seismosaurus* are writing papers and books about their discoveries and planning new experiments. Other scientists are building new instruments for looking under the ground.

Technicians will work for many years to get the sandstone off all the bones. When the work is finished, the bones will be kept at the New Mexico Museum of Natural History in Albuquerque.

Someday David Gillette and his excavators may find the rest of the skeleton. They know now that much of the *Seismosaurus'* skeleton was buried with the bones either still connected or else very close together. They may get help from the new instruments. If they are lucky, they may find the *Seismosaurus'* head. That would almost ruin the fun. What would they all do next?

Index and Pronunciation Guide

Boldface page numbers refer to illustrations